SURVIVOR STORIES

PLANE CRASH

True Stories of Survival

Frank Spalding

rosen publishing's
rosen central

New York

Published in 2007 by The Rosen Publishing Group, Inc.
29 East 21st Street, New York, NY 10010

Library of Congress Cataloging-in-Publication Data

Spalding, Frank.
Plane crash: true stories of survival / Frank Spalding. – 1st ed.
p. cm. – (Survivor stories)
Includes bibliographical references and index.
ISBN-13: 978-1-4042-0999-2
ISBN-10: 1-4042-0999-9 (library binding)
1. Survival after airplane accidents, shipwrecks, etc.–Juvenile literature.
2. Aircraft accidents–Juvenile literature. I. Title.
TL553.7.S675 2006
910.9–dc22

2006023341

Printed in China
On the cover: The wreckage of a passenger plane that crashed in Peru on August 23, 2005.

CONTENTS

Planes are often more likely to crash during takeoff and landing. This jet crashed into an airport warehouse during takeoff in Teterboro, New Jersey, on February 2, 2005.

INTRODUCTION

In the early days of air flight, planes were not widely used for travel. However, after years of great technological advances, commercial flight became a reality. Today, flying is generally considered to be the most convenient way to travel long distances. Journeys that once took days, weeks, or even months now take mere hours. The airplane has revolutionized transportation, and millions of people fly on airplanes every day.

Besides being convenient, today's airplanes are the safest mode of transportation in the world. Large jetliners are extremely safe, and the chance of being in one that crashes is roughly one in ten million. A traveler is far less likely to be hurt or killed on an airplane than in a car, boat, or train.

When airplanes crash, the results are often fatal. The best way to keep air travel safe is to make sure that accidents don't occur. To this end, many airplanes contain cockpit voice recorders, which keep a record of everything said between the pilot and the copilot during the flight. Airplanes also contain flight data recorders, which record information about the plane's speed, altitude, and location, among other things. These devices are designed to withstand extreme impacts, fire, water, and pressure. After a plane has crashed, cockpit voice recorders and flight data recorders can be retrieved and the information they contain studied. By figuring out what went wrong during a plane flight, aviation officials, airplane manufacturers, pilots, and engineers can make sure that it doesn't happen again. More than a century of air travel has ensured that modern travel is very safe indeed.

Safety features such as seat belts, life vests, and emergency exits can help save lives in the event of a crash. Most crashes occur when airplanes are taking off or landing, and most airports have emergency crews that can swarm upon the scene of the accident, extinguishing fires, extracting the injured, and providing medical care for the survivors. When crashes happen elsewhere, however, passengers often have to rely on their wits to survive.

1

ORDEAL IN
THE WILDERNESS

On September 20, 2004, a small, single-engine Cessna aircraft, piloted by Jim Long, flew over scenic Montana on its way to a small airfield in the Montana wilderness. Its passengers—Jodee Hogg, Matthew Ramige, Davita Bryant, and Ken Good—were employees of the U.S. Forest Service, a government organization that maintains America's abundant national forests. They were headed to Schaefer Meadows to conduct a survey of the trees and other vegetation in the area.

CRASH

It was early in the afternoon, but visibility was poor; the weather had been threatening all day. Suddenly, the small Cessna hit the side of a mountain. The plane had been traveling faster than 100 miles per hour (roughly 160 kilometers per hour) when it crashed through the trees. When it came to a stop, the plane was upside

The plane carrying Jodee Hogg and Matthew Ramige crashed near Glacier National Park. This rugged landscape of preserved wilderness would prove treacherous as they tried to find help.

down, and Hogg and her fellow passengers were dangling in their seats, held in place by their safety belts.

Long and Good sustained terrible injuries, but they were alive. Bryant wasn't moving. Before anyone could think of how to climb down to the ground, however, the plane burst into flames. Long immediately worked at freeing Good, who was sitting in the seat next to him. Good managed to climb free of the wreckage, but Long was not so lucky. Trapped in his seat, he would perish in the fire.

Hogg was able to free herself, and she made it out of the plane. She could have stayed outside, where it was safe but instead chose to climb back into the plane to help the other passengers. Ramige, who had sustained injuries in the crash, had difficulty getting out. Ignoring the heat, Hogg dragged Ramige out of the plane. Fed by the plane's fuel, the fire burned bright and hot. Hogg and Ramige moved away from the wreckage. They were high up in the mountains—high enough for snow to cover the ground. It was cold that high up, and it would only get colder once night fell.

Passing the Night

Hogg and Ramige made a crude shelter out of some wreckage from the plane. It was freezing cold outside, and Good crawled into the shelter with them. All three were hurt. Hogg had sustained burns, particularly to her hands, and had several sprains. She was in better shape than Ramige, however. He had severe burns to his face, neck, chest, hands, and thighs. He also had a broken back. Ramige could still walk but risked further injury, particularly to his spinal cord.

Good, however, had sustained the worst injuries. At fifty-eight years old, he'd been a member of the Forest Service for some time, and he was planning to retire at the end of the year. Hogg did the best she could to make Good and Ramige comfortable. As the chill of the night set in, she attempted to build a fire but was unable to. With no way to

When rescuers arrived at the wreckage they assumed that there were no survivors. The plane had crashed deep into the wilderness and it seemed unlikely that any survivor would be able to get far.

keep themselves warm, the survivors huddled together to ward off the cold. Unfortunately, Good succumbed to his injuries during the night.

Tough Choices

In the harsh light of morning, Hogg and Ramige realized that their chances of survival were slim. It had been hours since the crash, and there was still no sign of rescue. It was bitterly cold, and they didn't know if they should stay where they were or head off to get help. They decided to leave Good where he was. If they survived, they could send someone to recover his body.

Walking through the mountainous terrain was extremely difficult. As Forest Service employees, both were used to hiking. However, they had sustained serious injuries, especially Ramige. They knew they would have to focus on survival if he was to have any hope of making it through alive.

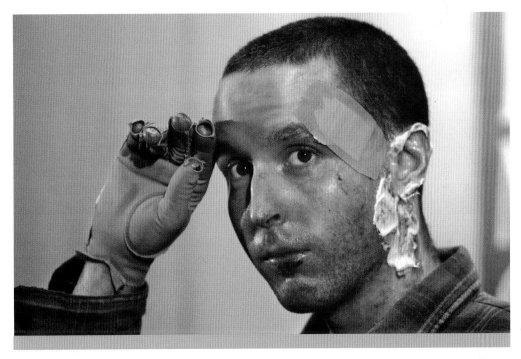

Despite his severe injuries, Matthew Ramige found the strength to walk through rugged terrain to safety. He is seen here not long after the crash, giving a press conference from Harborview Medical Center.

Leaving the crash site and pressing on by foot was a big decision. Rescue planes would be likelier to spot wreckage than two people walking. Ramige and Hogg hoped that, should the plane be found, rescuers could follow their footprints through the snow to wherever they were. Later in the day, however, the snow began to melt, erasing their tracks.

A MIRACULOUS RETURN

The plane had crashed on a Monday, and the wreckage was not discovered until the next day. The bad weather that caused the crash also kept search teams out of the air.

After the wreckage was spotted on Tuesday, a helicopter with a rescue team touched down. The rescue team hoped to find survivors but instead found the charred remains of the plane. The bodies of Long and Bryant were still in the plane, and Good was left lying outside. The rescuers didn't think it was odd that Good was outside the aircraft. Considering the violence of the crash, it was possible that he had been thrown from the plane.

It was clear that a very intense fire had raged inside the craft, burning anything that was flammable. Since nothing could survive such a fire, and since there were no footprints, the search was called off. Hogg and Ramige were not far from the site of the crash, valiantly trying to find someone to help them.

RESCUE

On their second day on the mountain, Hogg and Ramige finally came to a highway. The first few cars they tried to wave down didn't stop, but finally one did.

The two survivors were immediately taken to Kalispell Hospital, where they underwent examination. Due to Ramige's serious injuries, and the fact that his kidneys had begun to fail, he was airlifted to Harborville Medical Center in Seattle, Washington. He would have to undergo skin grafts and

An emotional Jodee Hogg attends a memorial service for her fellow passengers on September 26, 2004.

physical therapy. Ramige relocated to Albany, New York, to be near his family during his recovery.

That Hogg and Ramige managed to find their way to safety is a testament to their willpower and inner strength. Their families were overjoyed to learn that they had made it through the ordeal and were expected to make full recoveries. Their survival seemed like a miracle, especially considering that they had been reported dead.

2

THE SURVIVORS

Above and beyond all else, Ronnie Van Zant was a hard worker. Growing up poor in Jacksonville, Florida, during the 1960s, he was a tough kid who could have followed in his father's footsteps and become a truck driver. Instead, he discovered music. In time, he dropped out of school to focus on his new love. Van Zant didn't know how to read music and could barely play the guitar, but he had songs in his head and he could sing.

Gathering a bunch of younger musicians into a band, Van Zant applied his strong work ethic to creating rock 'n' roll. He knew what he wanted from his band, Lynyrd Skynyrd, and it gave it to him. Lynyrd Skynyrd slowly gained in popularity as it relentlessly toured the United States, and then the world. Van Zant's bandmates respected his integrity and charisma, and none challenged his leadership. Van Zant was so committed to the band's fan base that he kept Lynyrd Skynyrd on the road nearly all year round.

Allen Collins plays guitar while Ronnie Van Zandt sings at a Lynyrd Skynyrd concert in the 1970s. The band played so many concerts each year that they eventually had to charter a plane to travel to them all.

TOUR OF THE SURVIVORS

In 1977, Lynyrd Skynyrd went on tour in support of its latest album, *Street Survivors*. Although the band had used a bus on its previous tours, the members agreed that it made sense for them to get a plane, which would allow them to travel to gigs quickly and in greater comfort. To this end, they chartered a small Convair 240 airplane.

Twenty-five people followed Ronnie Van Zant onto the plane on October 20, 1977. Many of the passengers didn't have a good feeling about the pilots or the aircraft—one of the engines had a problem on the previous flight earlier in the day, causing a giant flame to shoot from the engine. Still, the members of Lynyrd Skynyrd were young and excited to play. Moreover, they had resolved that this flight would be their last on the rickety Convair. It would take them to Baton Rouge, Louisiana, for the fifth of eighty shows that they'd scheduled on the tour, which they had dubbed the "Tour of the Survivors."

DESCENT AND IMPACT

Spirits were high until a loud sound came from the right engine of the plane, which had suddenly, inexplicably, gone out. Keyboardist Billy Powell and drummer Artimus Pyle headed to the cockpit to talk to the pilots. The plane had suffered from other midair mechanical problems in the past, but each time the pilots had assured them that nothing was wrong. When the two men entered the cockpit and demanded to know what was going on, the pilots told them that everything was all right. But everything wasn't all right. A moment later, the other engine failed. A serious miscalculation had been made, and the plane was running low on fuel. The pilots informed everyone to get in their seats and buckle their seat belts.

A few minutes passed before the plane actually struck the ground. During this eerie stretch of time, the passengers had nothing to do except wait. (Many times, a plane can safely land even if its engines and landing gear aren't working properly.) It soon became clear that the plane was headed into a forest. The silence was broken as the plane crashed violently through the trees.

The impact caused the seats to tear free from the floor. In a high-velocity plane crash, everything inside of the fuselage is thrown

The wreckage of the Convair carrying Lynyrd Skynyrd came to rest near McComb, Mississippi. The seriously injured survivors of the crash had to be airlifted to a hospital in nearby Jackson.

forward. In many commercial flights, the interior of the plane is a strictly controlled environment. Luggage and other items are stored beneath seats or in overhead bins. Commercial flights also have teams of flight attendants who make sure that certain safety rules are followed.

Lynyrd Skynyrd hadn't hired any flight attendants, and the Convair's cabin was filled with unsecured items. As a result, the passengers were pelted by a number of loose objects. It's thought that one of these objects struck lead singer Ronnie Van Zant in the head, killing him instantly. Guitarist Steve Gaines and the pilots died instantly, too. Most of the people in the plane sustained extremely serious injuries.

GETTING HELP

Artimus Pyle was very badly wounded but managed to climb free of the wreckage. Many of the plane's passengers suffered broken legs. Luckily, Pyle did not.

Pyle's most significant injury was the compact fracture of his rib cage. With his broken ribs sticking through his skin, he set out in search of someone, anyone, who could help. He was joined by Marc Frank, a member of the band's road crew, and Kenneth Peden Jr., the sound technician. They walked through the forest until they finally came upon a small farmhouse.

The owner of the farmhouse, Johnny Mote, did not know what to make of the men coming toward him. Helicopters had begun arriving at the crash site and were shining their spotlights down. The men were covered in mud and blood. Thinking that the helicopters had been called out to look for escaped prisoners, Mote took out his shotgun and fired a warning shot. Some pellets from the shotgun blast hit Pyle in the shoulder, knocking him to the ground. The men quickly explained what was going on to the confused homeowner,

Artimus Pyle, seen here playing drums, suffered a serious compound fracture of his rib cage the night of the crash. He braved these grave injuries to look for help for the survivors.

who put down his gun. After making sure that Pyle was not seriously injured, they piled into Mote's truck and headed for the crash site.

A rescue crew arrived and assessed the situation. The conditions of the rescue were far from ideal—the ground was incredibly muddy, and a small crowd had already begun to form—but they still managed to get everyone to safety. The survivors were airlifted more than 100 miles (161 km) to Jackson Memorial Hospital in Jackson, Mississippi.

STILL SURVIVING

Followers of Lynyrd Skynyrd were shocked when they heard that Ronnie Van Zant, Steve Gaines, and Cassie Gaines had been killed. It seemed like the band was going to break up. The surviving members had a lot of healing to do before they were ready to talk to the press. In the meantime, funerals were held for the deceased. All over the world, their fans mourned.

In 1979, the remaining band members performed together again. They played one song at a benefit to an enthusiastic crowd. They would go on to play together in different bands and, eventually, put together a new version of Lynyrd Skynyrd with Ronnie Van Zant's younger brother, Johnny, taking over as lead singer.

3

SPY FROM THE SKY

The Union of Soviet Socialist Republics (USSR), also known as the Soviet Union, was once the largest nation in the world. Encompassing more than a dozen present-day countries, including Russia, the USSR was founded in 1922 and dissolved in 1991.

After World War II, the nation rose in prominence to challenge the United States for the title of the world's greatest superpower. The two had been allies in the war, but an economic and political rivalry developed between them. The United States was, and is, a country with a free-market economy, a free press, and freedom of speech. The USSR was a Communist country, meaning that the government controlled the economy and the press, and that people's individual freedoms were extremely limited.

In the wake of the destruction wrought by World War II, it seemed that either of these nations had the potential to shape the future of the world. Their old alliance long forgotten, both began to amass gigantic militaries. In addition, they began to stockpile nuclear weapons.

By the 1960s, this rivalry—which became known as the Cold War—had become very tense.

ESPIONAGE FROM ABOVE

Francis Gary Powers was born in a small Kentucky town in 1929. At the age of twenty-one, he decided to pursue a career in the military. After enlisting in the U.S. Air Force in 1950, Powers proved that he was born to fly. He eventually caught the eye of the U.S. Central Intelligence Agency (CIA).

The CIA is a government organization responsible for gathering information on foreign powers. The CIA had its hands full during the Cold War: the USSR was a huge, secretive nation that was, in many ways, closed to Westerners. It had a huge internal police force and intelligence agency, known as the KGB.

One of the CIA's most important tasks during the Cold War years was to gather information on the state of the USSR's military, specifically its nuclear weapons capability. To this end, the U.S. military developed the U-2 spy plane. The U-2 could fly at altitudes of more than 70,000 feet (21,336 meters), high enough that Soviet fighter planes could not engage it in combat. In an age before spy satellites, the U-2 was the United States' best hope of conducting secret surveillance of the Soviet Union. In 1956, Gary Powers was selected to pilot a U-2. He would go on to conduct

This image of Gary Powers and a U-2 is taken from a 2000 Berlin museum exhibition. The unique circumstances of Powers's plane crash made him a symbol of the Cold War.

espionage missions over the USSR, photographing Soviet military installations.

SHOT DOWN

On May 1, 1960, Powers was conducting an espionage mission over the Soviet Union when he was shot down by a surface-to-air missile.

The very fact that this happened was surprising—the U-2 was supposed to fly high enough as to be unassailable. Still, the designers of the plane had considered that such an event might take place. The U-2 was notoriously difficult to fly, and even if it had been impossible to shoot down, there was still the chance that the pilot might lose control of the plane.

Explosive charges were placed around the photographic equipment. To activate these charges and destroy this equipment, the pilot had only to flip two switches. This would prevent the Soviets from discovering what had been photographed. Because important mechanical parts of the plane would also be destroyed by the blast, the Soviets would also not be able to take apart a downed U-2, figure out how it was made, and design their own high-altitude spy planes. The explosions would go off one minute after being activated, giving the pilot time to eject from the plane.

Powers was equipped with a small, poison-tipped pin. In the event that a downed U-2 pilot was captured in enemy territory, he had the option of ending his life. Captured pilots would certainly be interrogated—and perhaps even tortured—by their captors. In order to spare himself the pain of torture, as well as to keep from divulging American secrets, Powers could use the pin to commit suicide.

However, when the Soviet surface-to-air missile shot Powers down that day, he had time only to eject from the plane. The U-2's canopy was fired off from the body of the plane, and a moment

Because he was unable to activate the U-2's self-destruct mechanism, the remains of Powers's downed U-2 were recovered by the Soviets. The wreckage was put on public display.

later, the rockets beneath Powers's seat fired, launching him straight into the air. Because the U-2 can nearly leave the earth's atmosphere, it's safe to say that Powers had quite a long trip down in his parachute. Powers didn't get a chance to activate the U-2's self-destruct mechanism, and he didn't kill himself with the poison pin. Soon after landing, he was taken into custody by the KGB.

Nikita Khrushchev holds aloft photographic evidence of the items found inside Powers's plane. The evidence recovered from the U-2 proved to the Soviets that Powers was, indeed, spying.

EVIDENCE

Nikita Khrushchev, the leader of the USSR, took a personal interest in the American spy. Dwight Eisenhower, the president of the United States, did not know that Powers was still alive. Because U-2s flew at such great altitudes, it seemed unlikely that Powers would be able to survive even if he had ejected from the craft. If he had, it was assumed that he would be able to successfully destroy all the sensitive information aboard the plane.

Under instructions from Eisenhower, the National Aeronautics and Space Agency (NASA) released a statement declaring that an American aircraft had disappeared. The agency did not mention that the plane had crashed or that it had been sent on an espionage mission.

Khrushchev was not amused. The next day, he made Powers's capture public, bringing the true story to light. Not only did the Soviets recover the plane, they also found Powers's suicide pin and the undeveloped film he had shot. After the film was developed, it was abundantly clear that Powers had been on an espionage mission. This was an awkward and dangerous development, and it had the potential to be politically disastrous for Eisenhower. Suddenly, it seemed that the Cold War was heating up. Further negotiations between the two nations did nothing to cool the temper of the furious Khrushchev.

TRIAL

While this international drama played out, Powers prepared himself to go on trial. Even after admitting that he was, in fact, a spy, the U.S. government would not formally apologize to its rivals. This move guaranteed that Powers would not be treated kindly by the Soviets.

Because he was a spy, Powers was classified as an employee of the CIA rather than an American soldier. This simple distinction meant that he would not be eligible for the treatment generally accorded to prisoners of war (POWs). Under international law, POWs must be treated humanely. They are usually sent back to their home countries when hostilities have ended, or traded for other POWs. Without these protections, Powers was at the mercy of the Soviet government.

It was August when Powers finally went on trial. Alone on the witness stand, he faced a large, packed courtroom. With the evidence stacked against him, Powers admitted that he had been flying over the USSR for the purposes of conducting espionage. However, he managed to avoid giving away any classified information.

This photograph of Gary Powers was taken shortly after he was taken into KGB custody.

At the conclusion of his trial, Powers was sentenced to three years in prison, followed by seven years of hard labor. This was bad news for the young American pilot. Soviet prisons were notoriously brutal, and hard labor camps could be even worse.

FREEDOM

Luckily for Powers, the U.S. government was eventually able to make a deal with the Soviets to exchange him for a Soviet spy in American custody. After serving nearly two years of his sentence, he was freed. Upon Powers's return to the United States, his actions in the Soviet Union were thoroughly investigated by a special committee. Eventually, he was found to have acted honorably under difficult circumstances. Officially, Powers was cleared of all suspicion. Nevertheless, doubts about his conduct lingered.

Powers died in 1977. During a routine day of work as a helicopter pilot, his helicopter crashed and he was killed. Twenty-three years after his death, and forty years after the U-2 crash, Powers's service to the United States was finally officially recognized. His family was awarded a number of medals, including the Distinguished Flying Cross. This is one of the highest honors that can be bestowed upon a pilot. It is only awarded to those who show exceptional heroism while in combat. It may have taken decades, but long after his death, Powers was finally recognized as a hero.

4

SURVIVAL IN THE ANDES

In October 1972, a Uruguayan rugby team called the Old Christians chartered an airplane to Santiago, Chile, for a competition. Although Chile neighbors Uruguay, the countries are divided by the Andes. A vast mountain range that runs the length of South America, the Andes are home to some of the highest peaks in the Western Hemisphere.

The chartered aircraft was a Fairchild F-227 that belonged to the Uruguayan air force. It was a small propeller plane that seated more than forty people. The young rugby players filled the remaining seats with acquaintances, friends, and family members.

A Difficult Decision

On the way to Chile, the plane made a stop in Buenos Aires, Argentina. The pilots estimated that the trip would take only four hours. However, they were worried about the final part of the trip, which would involve passing through the Andes. Some of the mountains in the Andes have peaks that are higher than 20,000 feet (6,100 meters). The Fairchild did not have strong enough engines to fly over the mountains, so it would have to fly between them.

After completing the first leg of the journey and landing in Buenos Aires, the pilots considered turning back. The weather had been bad, and they didn't want to put their passengers in peril. Moreover, they could not wait long in Argentina to see if the weather would improve. This left them with a difficult decision. After consulting with two Argentine cargo pilots who had just successfully flown through the Andes, the Fairchild pilots decided to go ahead with the trip. It was a decision that would cost them their lives.

DISASTER IN THE ANDES

On October 12, the Fairchild passed into a heavy fog bank as it entered the Andes, heavily reducing visibility. Trained to fly by relying on their instrument panels, the pilots were unconcerned.

Suddenly, the turbulence got a lot worse. The Fairchild was a light plane, and it was thrown around by the air currents. When the plane emerged from the cloud bank, everyone aboard realized that something had gone horribly wrong. Somehow, an error had been made, and they were flying too close to the mountains. Before the pilots could take evasive action, the right wing hit the side of a rock face. It broke free from the body of the plane and cut off the tail. Soon, the left wing was torn away as well. The crippled aircraft plummeted into the jagged peaks of the Andes.

Several people were in the tail of the plane and were killed when it broke away from the fuselage. Three others were sucked out the back of the craft. Luckily, the fuselage landed on a snowy incline and eventually slid to a halt. Two men were thrown from the fuselage, but the others managed to stay strapped in. When the Fairchild came to a halt, some of the young men went to work freeing those who were trapped

The survivors of the crash would find shelter in the Fairchild's fuselage. Stranded high in the Andes, they huddled together for warmth and fashioned hammocks for the injured.

in the wreckage. Three people had been killed instantly in the crash, and it became immediately clear that others had suffered extremely serious injuries. One man walked away from the plane in a state of shock. He wandered aimlessly through the snow and freezing temperatures and fell into a deep valley, vanishing from sight.

DAMAGE CONTROL

Three of the survivors—Roberto Canessa, Gustavo Zerbino, and Diego Storm—were medical students. Their training would prove to be invaluable. All of the rules had changed, and the survivors didn't know how long it would be until help arrived. Injuries that wouldn't normally be serious could be fatal if not attended to. It turned out that help would not be arriving for some time, and the knowledge that the medical students shared between them would be valuable for more than dressing wounds.

Most of the survivors had only mild contusions, but some had very serious injuries indeed. One young man had his leg cut off, another had a deep flesh wound in his calf, and still another had a badly broken leg. An older woman had been crushed by a number of seats that had torn free of their moorings. Unfortunately, the survivors were not able to free her.

As night fell, the survivors took stock of their situation. They were stranded in the middle of the Andes at an extremely high elevation, it

By working together, the survivors of the Fairchild managed to stay alive for more than two months in terrible conditions. Everyone was given a job to do. Even injured survivors helped out by melting snow to make water.

was bitterly cold, and some of them were badly hurt. With the injured made as comfortable as possible, the young men arranged themselves in the ruined fuselage and tried to go to sleep.

DESPERATION

Ten days after their crash, they still had not been rescued. A few planes had flown by but gave no indication of seeing the wreckage.

Several people had died from their injuries, and others were suffering from altitude sickness. The small amount of food scavenged from the plane was not enough to survive on.

Hungry and desperate, the survivors were quickly running out of strength. They were not sure where the valley they were in was situated, but they were sure it was near Chile. It seemed that someone would have to climb one of the towering peaks near the wreckage to survey their situation, but doing so would be impossible unless they could find some sustenance to build up their energy. One thing was for sure: the longer they waited, the weaker they would become.

Canessa's medical training made him realize that a dead human body had nutritional value. The survivors were disgusted by the thought of eating human flesh, but it was becoming clear that they would starve if they did not. Canessa cut some flesh from one of the corpses lying out in the snow and forced himself to eat it. Over time, the rest reconciled themselves to this grisly diet as well.

RESCUE EFFORTS

The minute that air traffic controllers realized that something may have happened to the Fairchild, they began contacting rescue services. Members of the Chilean air force took to the air in search planes, but it was generally assumed that everyone had died in the crash.

Flying through the Andes was dangerous even for the most skilled pilot. Anyone who braved the treacherous air currents of the mountain range was taking a very grave risk. Many people thought that it wasn't fair to ask rescuers to risk their lives searching for what were almost certainly dead bodies. Still, the air force was required to look for survivors for a reasonable period of time. Although Chile was undergoing drastic political upheavals, the air force did just that.

While the pilots were searching for the wreck of the Fairchild, the survivors' families waited desperately for good news. Worried about their children and loved ones, they wanted to do something, anything, to aid in the rescue efforts. Unfortunately, there was not much that they could do except stand by and pray.

Unable to help in the official search, some of the parents took matters into their own hands. One sought out a local man who was familiar with the mountainous terrain of the Andes, but it became apparent that traveling through the mountains by car was futile. Another consulted a supposed psychic.

The air force called off the search after eight days. All aircraft— military, commercial, or otherwise—were instructed to keep an eye out for survivors when flying over where the Fairchild was believed to have crashed. Even without the support of the government, the survivors' parents did not give up.

EXPEDITIONS

In order to figure out a way to get to safety, the survivors made several expeditions. They sent small groups out to determine the lay of the land. The survivors had learned how to make primitive snowshoes by strapping seat cushions to their feet, and they made sunglasses out of material scavenged from the planes.

As difficult and tiring as these expeditions were, it was clear that no one was coming to rescue them. On their seventeenth night on the mountain, an avalanche flooded the fuselage of the Fairchild, suffocating five survivors. Of the more than forty passengers, there were now only nineteen. Three others would later die.

On November 15, more than a month since the Fairchild had crashed, the final expedition set out. Antonio Vizintín joined Canessa and Nando Parrado. From the previous expeditions, they knew that they would need to dress warmly and build up their strength. They wore multiple layers of clothing against the cold and carried supplies, including blankets and extra meat.

They soon discovered the tail of the airplane. They found clothing, a little bit of food, and the powerful batteries that would run the plane's radio. They spent the night in the tail, and the next day decided to return to the Fairchild. If they could bring the radio to the batteries and connect the two, perhaps they could radio for help.

Unfortunately, after spending days removing the radio from the cockpit and dragging it all the way to the tail, they realized that they didn't have the technical expertise to get the radio working. They returned to the plane after eight days, deciding that it would be best to rest up before resuming the expedition.

CLIMBING A MOUNTAIN

With extra supplies, extra food, and rudimentary sleeping bags sewn from material taken from the plane, the three young men set off on December 12. They made their way up a mountain to the west, eventually spending the night sheltered by a boulder. The next morning, they clawed their way up the sheer rock face to the top of the mountain. But rather than the lush, green valleys of Chile that they'd expected, they saw only more snow and mountains.

Refusing to give in to hopelessness, they surveyed the terrain ahead of them. Seeing two mountains in the distance that were not covered in snow, Parrado plotted out a route he thought was likely to lead them to civilization. They estimated that it would take them more than a week to reach the mountains, so they sent Vizintín back to the Fairchild. With only two people, their food would hold out longer. Maybe long enough for them to get to the mountains.

RESCUE

It's hard to imagine what the shepherds who finally found Canessa and Parrado thought when they saw the two filthy, bearded, bedraggled young men on December 21. They had survived for more than two months on little more than melted snow and human flesh. They had climbed an extremely high and steep mountain and made their way through a valley, sleeping out in the open. The shepherds brought them to a nearby house and fed them a large meal of bread, cheese, milk, pasta, and meat. Some might have considered it simple peasant's fare, but for Canessa and Parrado it was a feast.

It didn't take long for help to arrive. The sixteen survivors of the Fairchild were brought to a hospital, where they made full recoveries. The young men made it home in time to spend Christmas with their families, who had never given up searching for them. To this day, the survivors of the Fairchild are remembered as heroes.

CONCLUSION

Although air travel is growing less dangerous with each passing year, it will never be 100 percent safe. The story of the Old Christians rugby team, as well as the other stories documented in this book, shows the harrowing experiences that plane crash survivors may face.

Robert Canessa *(left)* and Nando Parrado *(right)* ride behind Chilean police officers one day after their rescue. Canessa and Parrado helped lead rescuers to the remaining survivors, who were still on the mountain.

Whether the crash takes place on a remote mountaintop or behind enemy lines, those who survive the initial impact often have to count on their wits to stay alive. Even when the crash takes place on a busy runway where rescue efforts may begin within minutes, the ability of the passengers to think and act quickly can mean the difference between life and death. It is therefore no small wonder that as we offer our sympathies to those who die, we celebrate the miracle of those who survive.

GLOSSARY

altitude The height of an airplane above the ground.

altitude sickness The negative effects of having a decreased amount of oxygen in the blood, caused by the thin air found at high altitudes. The symptoms of altitude sickness can include shortness of breath, severe headaches, insomnia, nausea, and impaired thinking and movement.

canopy In certain types of aircraft, the canopy is the glassed-in area where the pilot sits.

capitalist Pertaining to capitalism, an economic system in which business and industry are privately owned.

charter To secure the services of a vehicle and driver.

Cold War A period of intense rivalry between the United States and the Soviet Union, lasting from about 1947 to 1991.

espionage The act of secretly gathering information, or spying.

fuselage The body of an airplane. The fuselage holds the passengers and cargo.

peril Danger.

surface-to-air missile A missile that is launched from the ground and engineered to destroy aircraft.

surveillance The act of watching over or monitoring.

unassailable Impossible to harm.

FOR MORE INFORMATION

International Society of Air Safety Investigators (ISASI)

107 E. Holly Avenue, Suite 11

Sterling, VA 20164

(703) 430-9668

Web site: http://www.isasi.org

National Air Disaster Alliance Foundation

2020 Pennsylvania Avenue NW, #315

Washington, DC 20006-1846

(888) 444-6262

Web site: http://www.planesafe.org

National Transportation Safety Board

490 L'Enfant Plaza SW

Washington, DC 20594

(202) 314-6000

Web site: http://www.ntsb.gov

U.S. Department of Transportation

Federal Aviation Administration

800 Independence Avenue SW

Washington, DC 20591

(866) 835-5322

Web site: http://www.faa.gov/index.cfm

WEB SITES

Due to the changing nature of Internet links, Rosen Publishing has developed an online list of Web sites related to the subject of this book. This site is updated regularly. Please use this link to access the list:

http://www.rosenlinks.com/ss/plane

FOR FURTHER READING

Draper, Allison Stark. *Fighter Pilots: Life at Mach Speed.* New York, NY: Rosen Publishing, 2001.

Holden, Henry. *Air Force Aircraft.* Springfield, NJ: Enslow Publishers, 2001.

Jarrett, Philip. *Ultimate Aircraft.* New York, NY: Dorling Kindersley Publishing, Inc., 2000.

Johnstone, Michael. *Look Inside Cross-Sections: Planes.* New York, NY: Dorling Kindersley Publishing, Inc., 1994.

Metcalf, Johnathan. *Flight: 100 Years of Aviation.* New York, NY: Dorling Kindersley Publishing, Inc., 2002.

Morris, Deborah. *Plane Crash and Other True Stories.* Waterville, ME: Thorndike Press, 2004.

Olsen, Larry Dean. *Outdoor Survival Skills.* Chicago, IL: Chicago Review Press, 1997.

Read, Piers Paul. *Alive: The Story of the Andes Survivors.* New York, NY: J. B. Lippincott Company, 1974.

BIBLIOGRAPHY

"Accident Investigation Factual Report." March 9, 2005. Retrieved
    May 2006 (http://www.fs.fed.us/fire/av_safety/mishaps/lessons_
    learned/n206sm_fact.pdf).

Associated Press. "Survivor Recalls Noise, Impact of Crash."
    Missoulian.com. Retrieved May 2006 (http://www.missoulian.com/
    articles/2004/09/30/news/top/news01.txt).

Associated Press. "2 Forest Service Workers Survive Crash."
    September 23, 2004. Retrieved May 2006 (http://www.fs.fed.us/
    rm/main/pa/newsclips/04_09/09_plane_crash/0923_newsday.html).

Ballinger, Lee. *Lynyrd Skynyrd: An Oral History.* Los Angeles, CA:
    XT377 Publishing, 2002.

Central Intelligence Agency. "Gary Powers." CIA.gov. Retrieved May
    2006 (http://www.foia.cia.gov/browse_docs.asp?doc_no=
    0000022308&title=GARY+POWERS+(RUSSIANS+DISPLAY-
    ING+U-2+WRECKAGE-AIRCRAFT+WAS+EQUIPED+W/+DES
    TRUCTO&abstract=&no_pages=0002&pub_date=9/12/1985&rel
    ease_date=9/12/1985&keywords=POWERS+G|U-2
    &case_no=F-1978-00488&copyright=0&release_dec=RIFPUB&
    classification=U&showPage=0001#details).

"Francis Gary Powers." Answers.com. Retrieved May 2006
    (http://www.answers.com/topic/francis-gary-powers).

"Gary Powers and the U-2 Incident." About.com. Retrieved May 2006 (http://americanhistory.about.com/library/weekly/aa061801a.htm).

Jamison, Michael. "Plane Crash Survivor Tells Story." Mountainsurvival.com. Retrieved May 2006 (http://mountainsurvival. com/talesofsurvuval/aircrash_montana/aircrash.html).

Jamison, Michael. "Stories of Heroism Emerge From Crash." Missoulian.com. Retrieved May 2006 (http://www.missoulian.com/ articles/2004/09/25/news/top/news01.txt).

Odom, Gene, and Frank Dorman. *Lynyrd Skynyrd: Remembering the Free Birds of Southern Rock.* New York, NY: Broadway Books, 2002.

Read, Piers Paul. *Alive: The Story of the Andes Survivors.* New York, NY: J. B. Lippincott Company, 1974.

Stark, Mike. "Miracle: Billings Woman and a Co-Worker Walk Out of Woods After Being Reported Dead." *Billings Gazette.* September 23, 2004. Retrieved May 2006 (http://www.billingsgazette.com/ newdex.php?display=rednews/2004/09/23/build/local/25-crash.inc).

Sullivan, Jennifer. "Plane Crash Survivor Recalls Struggle for Survival." Seattletimes.com. October 21, 2004. Retrieved May 2006 (http:// seattletimes.nwsource.com/html/localnews/2002068780_ ramige21m.html).

Sullivan, Michael. "Francis Gary Powers: One Man, Two Countries and the Cold War." Retrieved May 2006 (http://www.military.com/ Content/MoreContent1/?file=cw_fgpowers).

INDEX

ABOUT THE AUTHOR

Frank Spalding is a writer living in New York State. In the process of researching and writing this book, he developed a great amount of respect and admiration for the brave survivors of plane crashes.

PHOTO CREDITS

Cover © Yomona/AFP/Getty Images; p. 4 © Mario Tama/Getty Images; p. 8 © Raymond K. Gehman/National Geographic/Getty Images; pp. 10, 11, 13, 17, 23, 40 © AP/Wide World Photos; pp. 15, 19 © Neal Preston/Corbis; pp. 25, 28 © Carl Mydans/Time Life Pictures/Getty Images; p. 26 © Sovfoto; pp. 32, 34 © Group of Survivors/Corbis.

Designer: Tahara Anderson; Editor: Wayne Anderson
Photo Researcher: Amy Feinberg